salmonpoetry

Publishing Irish & International
Poetry Since 1981

the arts council
an chomhairle ealaíon

funding literature

artscouncil.ie

Silver Spoon

JESSAMINE O'CONNOR

Dear Susan,
Love your writing.
Keep well in Leeds
xx
Jessamine

With Illustrations by
Helen Chantrell

Published in 2020 by
Salmon Poetry
Cliffs of Moher, County Clare, Ireland
Website: www.salmonpoetry.com
Email: info@salmonpoetry.com

ISBN 978-1-912561-91-9

Cover Image & Internal Images: *Helen Chantrell*
Cover Design & Typesetting: *Siobhán Hutson*

Printed in Ireland by Sprint Print

Salmon Poetry gratefully acknowledges the support of
The Arts Council / An Chomhairle Ealaíon

Seán, Ashling and Ivy

xxx

for lighting up the world

Contents

Preface

When I first heard Jessamine O Connor read her work, I knew at once I was in the company of an unusually vital talent. There was an emotional voltage to her poetry that was compelling. There was raw honesty to her distilled storytelling and insights, with none of the linguistic flannel or grandstanding that too many poets favour. And there, at the heart of it, was the lived experience, in all its painful or joyful ordinariness, of a distinctive voice. I wondered whether that would transfer to the page with equal effect, but needn't have worried. Reading her work in this first full volume is to appreciate the immediacy of poetry that also gains by its textures – poems that strike for the nerve-ends, the ear and intellect, sometimes all at once. As editor of a magazine, *The Poets' Republic*, I read a diversity of poems from renowned to unknown creators, poems of wildly varying quality, style and form, and from every angled perspective conceivable. It's a rare delight when one of those poets' work makes the hairs on your spine bristle, and makes you covet the chance to be the first to publish it. Here's a poet who does that. Her huge-hearted salute to internationalism, 'Welcome', has instantly become one of my favourite poems. It's a piece of writing that should be pinned to every port's arrival gate; read aloud among schoolchildren; an antidote to insularity and the rationing out of humanity. It's a poem too, like much of Jessamine's output, that fuses the local and global, the personal, social and political, all in one big breath. 'Welcome' attests to the artistic clout of 'keeping it simple', which is not so simple a thing to achieve.

Here's what else distinguishes this poet's volume from many others on the packed shelves. She's a writer of insatiable observation, whose watchfulness of norms of existence – in the living home, the street, the doorways, the fields, her native heath, up a chimney, in a dog's glance – often lays bare its abnormality, or urges us on to revisualise the familiar. Telling lines – in poems such as 'Green', for instance – drill into memorable snapshots of experience. Innocence and menace interchange; fear and wonder collide. All this expressed, as is her knack, with unmistakeable lyricism and empathy. In a world and times where borders, fences and hierarchies are being reinforced and remilitarised, we need all the more voices speaking up to articulate the common cause of humanity. Jessamine O'Connor affirms the role of poet and poetry as crucial to that; her poems are its heartfelt and eloquent advocates.

NEIL YOUNG
Editor, *The Poets' Republic*

Welcome

the island speaks to refugees

I open up my craggy arms, my cliffs,
this shift of whirling gulls,
stretch my beaches wide,
reach out my hands
made of coral, stone and sand,
scatter islands like roses
or breadcrumbs, to show you
where to land

and when you're close enough
I'll lift up the rough cloth
of my hedges, fields and loughs,
wrap its patchwork cloak around you,
gather the lush green folds
and rolls of sequin blues
to make an earth cocoon
for you to grow in

because when you're rested
and ready to stir
it will be my pleasure
to watch your wings unfold,
unfurl in my cloud-thick hair,
sprout your new roots feet deep
into my lungs and feed me
your fresh air.

Crow's feet

Crow lands
on the blade
of my shoulder

clambers in brambles
cocks her beak –
   it's time

She picks
   small steps up
over my face

   gently for now
only shallow
     prints

curious scratches
she's finding
    her feet

There is all
   of our life
  for her

to pace
and claw my
  bread–white skin

    I inhale
the black fan
   of her feathers

let her
  softly prickle
my eyes.

Backcarrier

Offer me a lift
and I'm yours.
Present me
with your tipping hips,
the ridge of your spine

as I'm wrapped round
your ribs,
face pressed
into the beat
of your lungs.

Push us both
down and up.
Pedal us
to anywhere,
rock me

so the city wind
waters my eyes
forcing them shut,
so that all I can feel
is the sway and roll

of your body
carrying mine
through the dark
on the back
of your bike.

Hunting in the bathroom

Not for the first time, desperate
to prove myself sane,
knowing I wasn't wrong
by his relaxed eyes
pinprick pupils
and all the denials.

He was clean
he lied
sweat bubbling up from his hairline
and as it started to roll
I had to show it wasn't me
destroying us.

I lifted the lid off the cistern, checked every shelf,
fingers grey probing grimy cupboard corners,
I pulled the side out of the bath,
scattered the bin,
my reflection looked back frightened from the mirror –
could I be what he said?

In the gap under the washing machine
I squeezed a hand across, it brushed plastic.
Slowly nudged along the lino
they rolled out into the bathroom light,
half a dozen, maybe more
orange-lidded one-mil needles.

I let them lie there
and though it was expected
and the proof I needed
my blood just coursed faster, thicker
painfully, his face repeating on me
repeating, indignant, how I never believed him.

Kneeling, staring down, pulse pounding,
not knowing where to go if I ever got up,
my heart was hammering and trying to break out
and then it broke

and it broke

and it broke.

Line

We have blocked the line with caravans, a Mercedes bus,
    with the door come off
and a trailer draped in blanket, a child's rainbow-coloured
    tunnel inside it.

A pink plastic house sits on the track, a rotting woodpile
    long left to slime,
and a car parks there on and off.

Further along we sit around the firepit made of a tractor wheel
and on nights like the solstice look up at the stars and the
    rocketing sparks

feeling the ghost of a train roaring right through us.

My mother has never been old

People are always writing poems about mothers
in sepia tones, tannin stained from the teapot
or clouded by floury aprons,
limbs worn stout with scrubbing and kneading,
kneeling over kitchen floors
or the altar,
cream-coloured rosary beads
seen through the cracked light of distance
as something wryly meaningful; the writers
allow these women their religion and superstitions
but my mother has never been one of those,
has never been old
or old fashioned.

She is bright, diamond hard
and sharp, so the nostalgia I hold is for things like
her dancing late at night, not waltzes or two-step
but strutting to *Hot Legs,*
Brass in Pocket,
LA Woman.

Every flat full of books, records
spread onto the floor where I'd rescue and pore over
the sleeves, discovering newly for myself
the beauty and power of Janis, Jimi, Otis, and more.

There were no beads or religion, no kneeling,
she wouldn't even pretend to believe
to have things easier, no hiding behind excuses
like tradition
or enlisting her child in a church while complaining
that things never change.

She hands down wisdom, such as:
a girl should have opinions, voice them
and learn to defend herself,
reading is essential and cleaning can be a sign
of something being wrong, or worse, a dull mind,
and that your mother will always be in your corner
whatever corner you wind up in.

Sea swimmer, head climber, wine lover, writer,
grandmother; my mother has always been
miles ahead, walking purposefully
out of step.

Green

after Jacqueline Saphra's 'Hampstead 1979'

He has a wonky eye and a knobbly face
but is likeably attentive and not unattractive
whenever we end up next to each other, blathering
in the dregs of some house party or rave.

He's a DJ with nose-rings, stumpy dreads
and a gorgeous girlfriend who looks into my eyes
and tells me sweetly
how they are in an open relationship
and she knows we'll be good together –
but meaning me and him.

She leaves me leaning on the bar
with my pint of squash and headful of e's,
appalled.
I'm seventeen.

Notice

There's no memory in me
of Brighton Square, the half-house flat
my parents shared before the split

then just a shadow, time trapped like a camera flash,
of the garage me and mum stayed in
during transit, more a granny flat she says,
which her schoolfriend kindly lent us.

A stay in my granny's

before Brabazon Square, the cold corner of a terrace
with too many doors and the ghost
only I saw.

29 Little Mary Street, over an army surplus shop
beside Slattery's, and I can still see the silhouette of a rat
that sat in the bedroom door regularly, and being told to leave
when I was seen on the stairs – this was meant to be 'a student house'
meaning: no kids.

Back to granny's – then out again.
1 Ebeneezer Terrace, a corner house near The Coombe
and in that winter of '82 the snow flowed up to the sky
but I'd started school now, two bus rides away
– the first ever Educate Together –
so we had to move

to a different world,
the salubrious seaside, 71 Albert Road;
we shared the house with one other man, had a back garden
with grass like a forest canopy
but they were selling.

Staying by the sea, 12 Breffni Terrace,
the first in a run of basement flats,
a four-storey redbrick beauty of a house
but servant's quarters are gloomy
and the thumping of the landlord's family feet
across our ceiling was a torment
to me, always wanting to be up there
with them, playing, which I often was, until
the day of the smashed plates and tears
and then of course we got the four-weeks-notice
and they got divorced.

Some winter months in my stepdad's family home
while they were away

then a few doors down, another basement,
20A Summerhill Road, where the daughters above
loved knocking on our door
if it was only me there, and running off laughing
or else forcing their way in
to stare and sneer at my crappy room,
and I was terrified of them because – as they made clear –
this was *their* house.

Further up the same road, 3A,
steep steps down, not a lot of light and when
they were suddenly selling,
the auctioneer pushed his way past me into the flat
though I was alone and just thirteen.

Out to the sticks then, 32 Bayview Lawns,
a corner house on a strangely suburban estate, and we had it
for two whole years of my teens,
the walk to and from the Dart to school was a mile
along a harsh stony beach, perfect for smoking and self-absorption,
we chose to leave.

4 Longford Terrace, nice flat with a view of the sea
but the landlord had a daughter
who needed a place more than we did.

Out of home,
27 Lower Drumcondra Road
under the railway tracks, the bottom floor of a rotten house
that we affectionately called The Pit,
and while we were all dancing one morning
the prefab flat in the back burnt down gloriously
and later the landlord collected his insurance,
that tenant – by good fortune – being put out just beforehand

and around then I fell on my head;
a stay in The Mater followed by appointments,
more appointments and an ambulance chaser,
so though sometimes one eye looked back bigger than the other
the claim was in, and everyone grew impatient
in anticipation of the payout,
black mould over the bed, no heating, no hot water,
seven of us paid rent there for another year more.

8 North Frederick Street, a two-room flat at the back
with bars on the windows and a shower in the bedroom,
three of us in it until the landlord spotted my bump
and at eight months pregnant he called round to give me
four weeks' notice: this place was not suitable
for children, he said kindly, and him and his muscular son
with The Sun in his pocket
stood over me while I scrubbed at the carpet
trying to get the stains out that he said had cost me my deposit,
and I scrubbed with that belly nearly touching the floor
for 400 pounds and still didn't get it.

Carrying black sacks of our lives up the road
after finally finding a flat that would take us
but when I went in for rent allowance they wouldn't allow it,
this place too was unsuitable, they say calmly
but I'm hysterical, all the way back there
to pack up again, almost on the due date
and with no idea where we were going

but someone was moving out from a nice corner house;
27 Primrose Street, and she had a kid too so it would be cool
and for a while it was,
but the mould soon grew on the wall,
gas heating we couldn't afford to use
but the glass coals looked nice with the light on behind them
and we had problems that had nothing to do with walls.
Though before the end of that four weeks' notice
a skip appeared with the last of our stuff thrown in it
while we were out, the locks changed, and I wept for weeks
over a Moses basket I had wanted to keep.

More fortunate than many, my son and I
were offered back out to the seaside by my mother and husband
and stayed over a year in their two-bedroom flat,
his father soon becoming my ex –
that same night leaving the couch he was surfing
to sleep on the streets, in and around Stephen's Green mostly,
so we'd go in nearly every day on the DART to see him
and to see him decay.
Pushing the pushchair with dread up the road
craning to get a sight of him first, to wave,
wait til he got up off the cardboard at least
before the pushchair got closer, then one day
we're walking along
nearing another man curled up in a doorway
and my two-year-old boy calls out with joy
there's Daddy!

and coming back to that flat,
12 Eden Park, the best yet,
bay windows, no rent-rise or notice
just an incredible lonely view of the sea,
and then my money came through,
the head injury paid off
and we were gone
into the West

and it took years
to learn we can paint the walls, put up shelves, pictures,
or take them down, grow food, shift things around,
that it's allowed – no one is coming to throw us out.

So my children don't know what it's like yet to move, be insecure,
to not know where you're going to be, or for how long,
to keep everything always half unpacked –
but I will never forget.

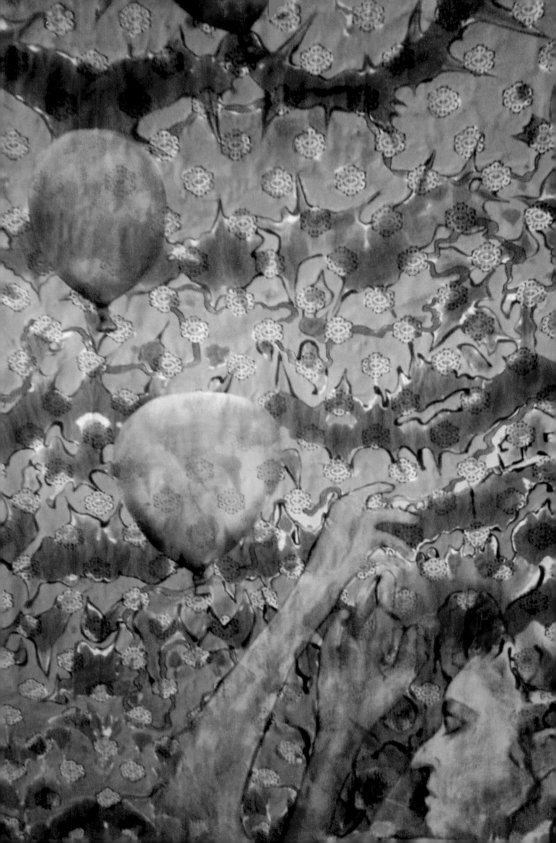

then down, feeling the flesh
of your arm
coming off the bone,
loosening under your cardy

Wishing you weren't deaf,
because all I can say
I can only say
with my hand
and this might be the last time
and you are pretending
to sleep.

Watershed

Learning to live in the world
we live in, without drowning,
means choosing canned laughter
over *One Day in Gaza*
because it's nine o'clock
and learning to live, to sleep, means that

It means no news at night,
no documentaries
about airstrikes, refugee camps
or hereditary poverty,
no children growing in rubble or dinghies
drooping into turquoise seas

Learning to live means avoiding history,
current affairs,
any futuristic programming
and definitely steering clear of climate,
topsoil, bees
and language

Learning to sleep
means closing your eyes
to the world
at night.
There is all day
to scream.

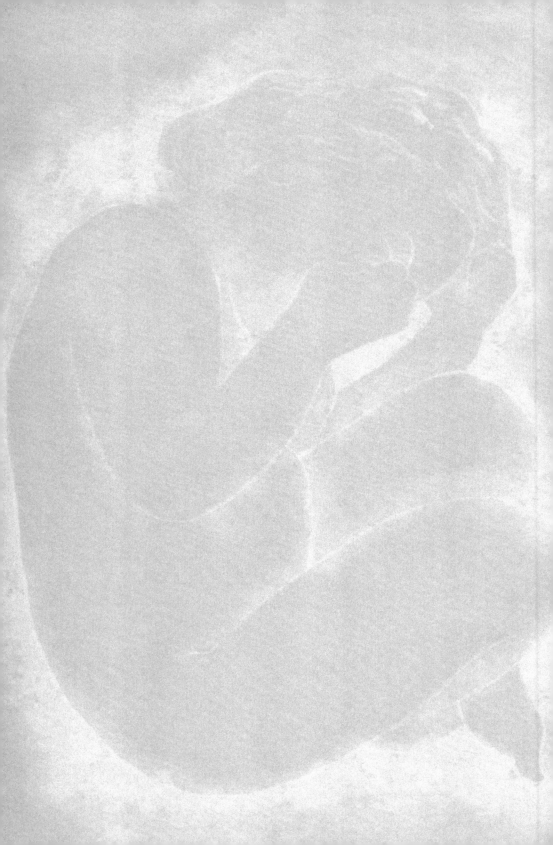

Christmas list for my newborn girl

Botox
vajazzles
spray tan
collagen

foundation
blusher, shadow
liner, stick-on lashes
anti-perspirant, perfume
body spray, deodorant, facelift
tummy tuck, magic knickers
padded bra, corset
silicone implants
waxed legs
shaved armpits
plucked eyebrows
a Brazilian, detox, diet
diet, diet, teeth whitening
anal bleaching, liposuction
colonic irrigation, pedicure
manicure, laser hair removal
cosmetic gynaecology

How long should
we leave it
before telling her
she mustn't
be perfect
after all?

When I grow up

When I grow up I want to be nobody.
I want to say all the same things as the people around me.
I want to believe whatever everyone else believes
and be happy enough with the way things are,
however they are.

When I grow up I want to be fashionable.
I want to throw away my clothes every season
and wear what's new.
I don't want to think about who makes the clothes, or how young,
    or exhausted,
or mistreated they are, I want to be cool.

I want to upgrade my phone just when I get used to it,
want to drive a new car, or at least have a new number plate.
I do not want to look like some weirdo in an old banger,
    wringing her hands
about aluminium mines and the oil industry,
I want to just drive.

When I grow up I will not age.
I want to own shelves and shelves of cosmetics, all tried and tested
    on rabbits
and pigs, just so I'm sure it will work on me.
I'll hide behind a skin-toned wall and paint on the mask, whatever
    way's the way at the time,
so no one would know I was somebody different, I want to be them.

When I grow up I want a house you could eat your dinner off.
The kind you walk straight out of and no one would know you'd
    ever lived there.
I don't want any books on the walls, blocking my annual
    catalogue paint-job,
and I'll be so busy tidying I won't notice the day passing,
or the years.

When I grow up I want to be married to someone presentable.
I want to wear a diamond ring, and be proud of those children
who waded in mud twelve hours a day mining
and dug with huge shovels, in blood and gunshots,
just to make my ring possible.

When I grow up I want to go to McDonalds, or KFC, or wherever.
I don't want to be a bleeding heart
animal lover
tree-hugging nutter.
I want to eat shit.

When I grow up I want to sit on the fence.
I'll never argue or make a scene,
I won't be protesting warplanes or boycotting Israel, that stuff is for loonies
who still think little children are worth more than money!
I won't complain.

When I grow up I won't think about things too much.
I will look blank if anyone tries making me care.
I will not be drawn
into some emotional reaction over the Earth,
I will be detached.

When I grow up I want to understand
why the economy is more important than water,
why fracking companies can tell all those lies,
but I want to believe them,
and when I grow up they will be right.

I want to live a long life with no scandals.
I want people to say over my grave that I was decent,
never made any trouble or a show of myself, that I kept things nice.
I want them to walk away talking about something else already.
I want to fade from memory, to have made no waves.

I want to be nobody. Nobody special.

Six hours

She's perfect

She glowers

She groans

She grunts and snorts

She drools slime into her ears

She has two long hands
and matching purple feet

She has a round nose
      the texture of eggshell
            decorated with white spots

Her eyes are dark and unconvinced

She likes to roll her tongue around

Stick her fingers into her face

And she wears my blood in her hair

ASIMO on prime time TV

Asimo, performing to adoring sighs, like a communal child.
You carried out a tray of drinks, trod down steps
and ran – actually ran.

You danced with the guest, soulless,
but everyone agreed you outdid her with your mechanical moves,
programmed to seem servile, dancing on screen

Running across the stage while the audience *oohs*,
delighted, letting themselves play the proud parents,
the presenter even called you *He*.

What I see is how fast you can run
and how those hands are so easily swapped for guns, or needles,
or spray, or voltage – how long are you going to stay four-foot-three?

Your dance is the decoy, the wooden horse.
They cheer and let you in, suppose you will be their pet
and dance all day carrying trays.

Of course they say you'll do the jobs we don't want.
As if a million-dollar-man like you will ever be wasted cleaning loos
or down an aluminium mine

Or picking over smouldering plastic
to find pieces of reuseable metal
like our children do.

Your act is faultless, your cracks invisible.
I watch and feel low level dread, a crawling tension
tangling round my stomach and chest

And you're hiding something we can't see yet,
all these antics for our amusement, like we're fed up of humans
who can do what you do but so much better

Even my toddler dances better than you,
because she hears, and feels, and is moved by music
and it's not a programmed response but a rush in her ears.

I hate it but I ring with fear – emotions I have, you wouldn't know –
I also have imagination; like I find you, shut down in a box maybe
and smash you with some heavy thing left nearby accidentally

Or clip you and pull out your wires with pliers which I've had
    the foresight to bring
or just drive straight into you, goose-stepping down the street
in the future when you don't dance anymore.

I can feel these things my pet and an awful lot more.
What is it you do again, when you're not playing the puppet,
distracting everyone on prime time TV?

To The Oxford University Press

regarding the updated Junior Dictionary

You've taken the world around us away,
surrendered it all for a virtual world

A dictionary teaching children that trees,
birds, and a whole fieldful of grass
are not really real

Illustrating, by elimination,
that nature has no value and is not worth keeping

What matters now is Chatroom,
Blog and Celebrity,
and what would a child do with a Conker anyway?

A Buttercup can't tell you anything
about the lactic tastes of an iPod
and no one climbs Beech trees
or gathers Hazel nuts these days

      or so you must hope

because you've hidden the words
where children can't find them

So when they go searching for an Acorn
or Bluebell, or Newt,
they'll discover that those things don't exist anymore;

Their inheritance
is Cut-and-Paste,
Block-Graph and Voicemail

You inform them that a Blackberry is not sweet with juice,
but hard
and demanding
and needs to be bought

Colony

after J. Burnside's 'Erosion'

The thicket, thick with blackbirds,
sparrows, wrens and hedgehogs,
robins and a badger family

is being cleared
by my new neighbour.
I haven't seen her, but she's coming.

The fine big house she planted
there where the field used to be,
needs garden, not an untidiness of trees.

The JCB is in.
Its teeth rip into the roots and burrows,
it gorges on bushes and brambles

and spits them out.
There is no pause or warning.
There is no stopping.

The digger-man has earmuffs on
so he doesn't have to listen,
after all he's only pushing levers.

By evening the thicket
is a broken tangle,
dragged to the back field and set on fire.

The screams from cracking ribs and lungs
can't be heard
over the drowning din of diesel.

In a few weeks she visits,
patrols the new territory
in a colonialist hat

proudly mowing down
the first fresh blades
of her new lawn.

The planter

He's here now, digging the hole for me,
planting the oak, banking it up,
stamping down mud with unlaced boots
and we're cackling over something
I will never remember.

Laughing now at the tree, that reaches up
into power lines which were always overhead,
and every few years the maintenance men come
to cut it short, and he's been dead
for almost as long as I've known him.

At the seaside

Small boy throwing stones
into a wide blue sky,
he scoops quickly, watching
as the first ones fall.

Into a wide blue sky
he pitches arcing armfuls,
as the first ones fall
the sun is bright in his eyes.

He pitches arcing armfuls,
watching them watch him,
the sun is bright in his eyes
as the tank starts slowly turning.

Watching them watch him,
long gone beyond fear,
as the tank starts slowly turning
he flings freely – just one more.

Long gone beyond fear
he scoops quickly, watching.
He flings freely. Just one more
small boy, throwing stones.

Django in the white clover as the swallows fledge

There's a hole in the house where my dog used to be.
The vet came and asked did I want her to leave
but I said no.

All morning rubbing his ruff,
stretching his ears,
stressing to him how good how good how good he was.

The first time in a year he walked ahead of me
on the lane, snorting and ploughing
into the straggly grass and buttercups

My eyes pouring watching him
rolling the last of his smell into pillars of flag iris,
then back on the step, feeding him boiled rashers from my
greasy fingers.

Django, lying out on the platform like he's waiting.
Me sitting, dreading the sound of a slowing engine
which doesn't come for hours.

So we wait together.

Django under the swallows' nest, in the white clover,
the day they're fledging.
The parents rocket and shriek around us

Swooping the dome-blue sky with angular wings,
shaking the beech leaves,
and the racket, everywhere.

One after another the young topple out,
fall, flap, dip, climb, and try to land on the old telecom wire,
trying and missing, they roll in the air.

We watch them devoutly and count. How many left now?
Stroking his old soft head,
waiting for the crunch of a car.

Féis

The girls across from us are used to this.
The small ones huddle, slurp straws, lick salt off their crisp fingers,
absorb each other's uniforms.

The bigger ones idle in tracksuits for now,
displaying a disconcerting expertise
with face-paint and eyelashes.

The mothers circle their stools
around small tables they fill and refill with dinner plates,
lattés, and bottles of coke.

It's February and the tans are alarming.
I can't take my eyes off this one woman's arms,
a rich red cheddar glow, and I stare

as she wrenches the hair off her children,
scraping and pulling their heads while they wince,
though she's not even looking.

Craned back talking to the women behind her,
she pulls out a huge canister and fires it
straight into each little face she's tugging.

The girls, clearly expert, expect when to brace
for the spurt of spray, know to shut their eyes,
and not breathe in the heavy metal cloud.

In the mist of this the teens vaporise,
and reappear day-glo monsters,
nests of nylon hair pinned into their heads

cheeks pink as aunt sally dolls,
milk white socks and sour faces.
The mothers praise the transformation,

specially the tallest girl,
who now bounces a headful of blacker than black
corkscrew curls.

Wonder Woman impersonator,
my daughter whispers.
The hours pile up, they get their pound of féis.

Scan

Alien inside, spooky grey on the screen
All squirming bones and hollow eyes
Growing in the dark
Stamping out a space for itself
In the warm igloo of my insides

As my neck lies twisted towards the monitor
It rolls away, turns a bony back to us
The scan lady laughs, freezes the moment
The cold shoulder
I recognise instantly the child of my lover

Great

Banging the drum,
the bloodbath remembered
now in slow motion sepia
reconstructions

Boys and men smart
in starched uniforms,
stoically going up and over,
charging on as ordered

Their annihilation shown on screen
as fluttering petals,
poppies gorged red
fed on young men's blood

It's time again to cull the poor
so make them some costumes,
make up some story,
and send them off killing each other,
just call it war.

Three new fathers

Ten days late.
You don't go for the taxi.
After a little rest, you smile,
and gouge on the bed.
Eighteen hours later
you're proud, you'd love another
but now you have to get going,
can't leave it too late.
You leave us alone
on a ward full of fathers,
wishing I could stitch
shut the curtains around us.

*

Three weeks late.
I drive myself in.
All through it thinking
someone will tell you
and you'll appear at the glass,
poison the staff,
hold the white pillow
down into my face
and tear up the baby.
I beg and beg them
to let me out,
before you get in.

*

One day short of two weeks over.
You drive fast.
There's no panic, I grit
every four minutes.

I send you for food,
and you sit behind me chewing
while I pant on the bed,
overwhelmed in sweat.
Have you not finished
that bloody roll yet? I spit.
You rub, and don't rub,
do as you're told.

I stroke and kiss your hand
then crush it,
roar, and push her out,
just like that.

Meet me for coffee

Not a cup of tea, a pint or just 'meet me'
because I want to wait awkward at a counter beside you
with the steam spluttering, the espresso machine knocking
and our overdressed elbows almost touching

I want to sit opposite you at a small table
that can never be small enough, absorbing the heat
of your hidden knees and then eyes when I catch you
watching me lick the froth off my lips

I want us to be both fiddling with our round white cups,
thumbing the holes that make the handles,
intense with conversation while idling our fingers
around and around those curves

I want to be alone with you in a clamorous place
where no one will notice what's not being said,
that's why I say safely, meet me for coffee,
instead of suggesting something else.

Silver spoon

I don't know what to do with the spoon
Found, now, at the back of the drawer
Five old silver spoons bound
Together in an elastic band

But this one, the black one, slid in there
Hidden there
And I know it was me, thinking
I was being clever, that put it there

So it's surfaced now, blackened and filthy
Scorched by history, sudden and smoky
Hideous, but held out in the kitchen light
I nearly don't want to let it out of my sight

   You are old times
   You are a thousand different moments that were all the same
   You are a time capsule with my youth perched inside, grinding
   You are magnetism
   No one I know now knows what you mean
   You are still in my hand
   My thumb rubbing your length
   And you, the way you feel pressed in my palm

Following down
My forearm is white, unmarked
Except for the flowers, untracked
Intact, delicate, suddenly precious

The tiny pink petals seem to curl brown
In the curved shadow of the spoon
Still held up to the light of the room
In my deceptively steady right hand

The furniture rights itself,
and all the ransacked things go back
to where they were, when they were hers.

Rocks and pebbles start to rock then roll
and thump down dust-spraying stairs,
through the hall,

and outside, the paint regenerates,
bubbling from shutters
and fascia

like fuchsia, blooming,
a fresh fleshy pink, like a new baby,
like when it was new.

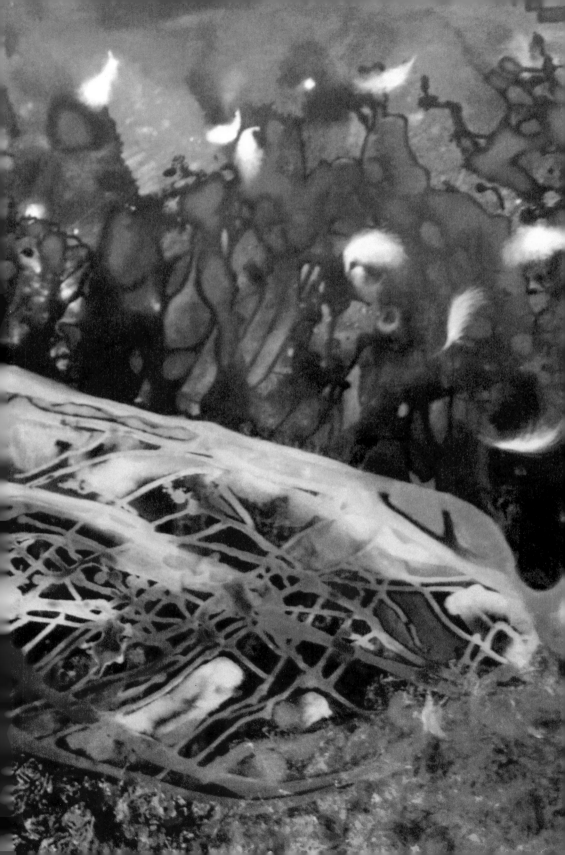

Sleepless Lough Gara

In the dark
the lough is singing

A glockenspiel choir
of arctic geese

Squeezing through
the bedroom window

Easing bubbles
of orb notes gather

And drift in clusters
across black space

Ballooning nearer
the music bursts

A snowstorm of feathers
melts on my face

There was no funeral

There was no funeral in the bathroom
when her first unborn slipped into the toilet
unnoticed. So when ten days later, still doubled over,
she was sent for the scan
to confirm she was clean – nothing left
to be infectious – and a nurse snarled the accusation
there's no baby here
as if she was pretending to be pregnant,
there were to be no condolences.

There was no funeral in the bathroom
the second time when she had already
live children to care for
and though the ambiguous twelve-week-old
foetus was leaving her, desolate,
there wasn't a suggestion of bereavement
counselling, or call for a priest, just painkillers
and an awkward handful of tissues
on the way back out the door.

There was no funeral in the bathroom
the third time when it had been her decision,
just a secret ceremony of her own,
blessing the first specks of it
the day after taking the pills,
and it is possible
to be both grieving and relieved,
knowing that this loss was no worse
than the others
where no one came to sympathise either,
or judge.

Pact

Eventually the crows stop building brittle knitted towers
in the chimney, and I miss them.

I miss their dawn scratchings, the feel of their feet
on the slates of my head, the crack
of tumbling bolts and glass on the apex roof
and the raucous chat, roaring
down our megaphonic chimneystack.

I miss their eternal silhouette standing guard on the pot,
on the house, over me, underneath, dislodging their foundations,
whispering up our secret.

Carraroe runaway

for Clare

If anyone asks, I'm not here.
I'm back in the shadow of limpet bristled limestone
burying my feet in the sand,
watching pink toes wriggle like strangers
and then packing them down with my hand
for the satisfaction of seeing the cracks break through.

If anyone asks, I'm busy
hands on knees hinged over, stood where the sand sinks,
I'm calculating the time x weight x tide ratio
to shriek when the beach gets a bite of my leg
and gasp at the suck of released feet
before starting the calculations again.

If anyone asks, I'll be back
but not until the sun has gone cold
and we've run out of sandwiches,
only when the purple anemone stop waving
and all the empty crabs and mussels and razors
have been licked into sand.

A skyful of kites

Children tumble into a sun-dried day,
scuffling up dust, chasing a ball,
mothers quietly watch them play
in the stretching shadow of the wall.
Its concrete knife cuts through the sky,
carving wide, beyond their sight
and when the sun sets, on the other side,
they are left holding only the fall of night.

They know well the sound as neighbours die,
have felt the shaking of walls, and fright,
corralled in this pen, kept from the sea
until, released by sleep, they fly –
small tangled fingers clutch one giant kite.
It lifts their dreams and carries them free.

Snowbird

after Mary Noonan's 'In the House'

If I had known, I would have said goodbye years before

Not at the artificial grass graveside
or the airtight TV room where you all sat like stuffed animals
but at your table, over the paintbrushes

Or on the coral strand, between sandwiches,
between swims, where I wallowed in the shallows
and admired your distant bobbing head trawling the horizon

Long before the vaporous woman seeped into you,
every year swelling, squeezing more and more out
until there was only an occasional glint, or a short sharp smile

There, up the powdery path, against your redbrick wall,
when you unclipped and lifted me from your daughter's bike
and held me high over your face, naming me Snowbird

It should have been then. If I had known, it would have been then.

Watch

I am growing again
The same long face
Strong nose
Ellipse lips
The curls
Not as firm
But sprouting in rain

The scowl
The stocky height of me
The bright of me
When I was her age
My youngest
The first face that I see
Myself in

I watch
Watch that no one
Ever
Knocks her down

Regular

That's the silver spoon in her mouth
has her talking like that,
he smirked
irked at how she'd knocked him back
and dressed it in words
he only half heard
over the banging of the band
and music so loud they'd both had to shout.

She took away her drinks from the bar
and sat back down
with her friend again.
He watched with a frown,
drank his pint nice and slow
and when she went out for a smoke he followed.
Later, untangling her hair from his hand
he wondered if he'd gone too far.

Morning radio

Two jackdaws pace the scaff planks outside
Pulling at things in the topsoil pile

      A father and daughter on a beach in Cork
      Gone from the farm

Dislodging roots
Abandoning the hill for the ground

      She was washed up
      He turned up later in the shallows

They stroll the gravel
Idly finding seeds

      Who brings a child swimming
      At midnight?

We keep our eyes intently
On the silvering birds.

Fog

My dog is fading.
Less and less I see his zebra print corner,
feel the warm weight of his head on my legs
or trip over his shadow sprawled in a doorway.

In the mornings now
the day only opens to a dropping robin;
his twiggy stride, his ruffed chest, his eyes
one at a time waiting for a sign to come in.

He blinks onto my boot.
A flitter and he fills the porch, territorially,
looking back at me, outside the door
being slowly eaten by fog.

The stranger

1.

Will I always be the stranger,
is that who I am?
Can I ever be at home
in this town?
It's too big to be this small.
I reach out with my hands and smile
but the road's too wide,
the wind is too strong.
I reach out
    and out
but you're gone.

There's a wall

but it's safe, or safer than home
or what used to be home, back
across the sea, though everywhere is across the sea
from here. The sea or the ocean.
I came by plane of course; hours of darkness
high over the water
suddenly becoming a vivid chessboard
underneath, a hundred greens,
all the shades that can be made
of rain.

I come from the City of the Drizzle
so I like it here, the rain, the grey,
and people are friendly
obviously, but
there's a wall
in the friendliness,
bricks I can't see.
Maybe they're glass,
ice,

made of space
or other invisible things
like history, DNA,
dreams,
I don't know.

We talk all the time, have good conversations
in the shop or outside, we laugh a lot,
I like them
but I've never seen
the inside of their kitchens.

So every week
at least, I text message home,
or where I'm from,
to receive by reply the noise
of voices, the city and heat
scrolling as characters
through my hand, letters spelling their sounds,
painting the lips
that would speak in my ear
if we could sit close,
breathing and laughing.
I almost see the flash of their teeth as I read, still
I tell my family, my friends, I'm doing well,
things are good
and they are,
it's fine,
quiet,
that's what we say – it's always quiet –
and I haven't decided
if that's what I want yet.

This main street
is as wide and empty
as the distance between us,
every week it gets wider.

But my dog is bilingual!

and I love learning English,
it's such a pragmatic language; the sounds of the words
carry the meanings inside them,
like suitcases
or baskets,
and it's safe here
I agree,
nodding my appreciation. I always smile
and text across the ocean, to say it's safe,
I'll stay
and be the stranger here.
Everyone's a stranger somewhere.

But will you always look at me the same way?
If I get all the sounds down
and mimicked perfectly to be more like you,
every vowel as lowing as your cows,
my consonants indistinguishable,
when my children are your children
or grandchildren,
when we're in the same graveyard,
maybe then

you'll call me local – what does it take,
ten years
or a millennium?
And must I always be grateful
for your coldness, your grey
and your spit
when I walk in our streets?
Have I got to repeat
the same thank yous
and how nice it's meant to have been to meet you,
forever? When can I stop
pretending
to not question anything?

Or be allowed to complain
about Ireland
like you do – without being accused
of telling people how to run their own country.
How long should I work here
before earning
an opinion?

    2.

I am new to this parish
of skyscraper and strangers,
new to this, new here
but I'll learn
and these towering buildings
will be my horizon
soon, when I call this place home, this eternity
of electricity, this terminal lack of night,
this city.

More people live in my apartment building
than our whole home town
and I know no one
and no one knows me – yet – it's liberating
so don't miss me,
don't wish I was back,
though sometimes I wish that.
I'm staying – at least for now anyway.

The journey wasn't bad,
I Skype home and we smile
in stop-motion moments, assuring each other
everything's fine, it will be,
I'm busy,
there's always something to do
or to look for
or look forward to.

But the sky is empty
because it's so bright
you can't see out of it, empty but alive
with human activity, busy,
heavy with helicopters, drones and planes,
buzzing and cluttered
so that there's no space beyond it.
The city
is like a pit of gravity
nothing escapes from.

In sleepless nights I stare up
        and up
but can never find them:
there are no stars here.
They must all be at home
stretched out
arms wide
legs loose
over the bog.
I miss them, can I say I miss the stars?
and the rushes and the puddles and the shitcaked cows
and the way you get away with nothing
and the miserable looking faces in the shop
on Sunday mornings, and all the relations you're tied to
but don't really know
living somewhere nearby, all the funeral handshakes
and wedding blackouts and talk about weather,
the tiny scandals and endless chatter –
who was in the new car
or back to their old ways –
can I say I miss all that
but I don't miss home?
Can I say I miss the stars?

3.

Ireland was a childhood dream,
I can't explain it
just always had the feeling
something important would happen here,
and I don't know if that thing
has happened yet
but I'm glad I came.
When I go home
it's like time has stopped.
I like the sensation of things going forward
but going back
is going backward,
and I know it isn't perfect here
but it's still lovely, lonely, everyone says hello,
they seem to like me
but none of them know me.

I think I'm good friends with my barber
and we always say we'll go out for a drink
or do something, sometime,
but we never do.
He's busy.

It's hard to make friends.

There's a wall.

When I bring my partner over to visit,
my mother is going to be so funny –
they are as bad as each other, neither speak
the same language
so my mother will shout,
that's how she understands how to be understood:
shout slowly!
Maybe they'll play Pictionary.

The best thing about English is
there is no gender –
which makes sense, I mean really
why is there ever? Who decided if a knife is a *She*
or a fork is a *He* – it's crazy!
Figuring out how to get on
in a new place, with new ways and strange food,
knowing no one, being misunderstood, *plus*
learning a language
is difficult enough,
without worrying
about things like

should this door be wearing lipstick?

One last beat

She   knows
The air   quivers
Dust mites   are raving
The dog's matte   fur is ecstatic
She hopes they don't notice, not yet
that her valves have stopped opening
while the children's bickering still
bounces harmoniously against the
sun-stroked crowded windows
tattooed with paw prints
The small house is
a paper lantern
they will all
outgrow
All but
one

My house

This was the last look at the land,
here where they stood in the wind
and waited, looking down the bog
impatient for a plume of steam
blooming along the narrow-gauge track

for the doors to open and shut
them in, on the way to the junction
with the big city line,
they say they'll be back
and don't know yet it's a lie

waiting, pacing, lifting cases,
hoarding in their eyes
the light off the lake,
the way the trees sway,
and all the softness of hills, birds and sky

carrying their cargo inside;
the entirety of life, who they are,
into the trembling train and away,
far across seas, roads and cities,
into new lives, old age, and death.

For many, here was the last place they left,
waiting on this platform
for change to come, some giddy,
some grieving, leaving
home.

Notes on poems

Notice, p20
List of places I lived before moving west aged 22. I was told to write it by my friend Siobhán who's involved with the Dublin Tenants Association.

Brothers, 7th May 1916, p29
Composed from a document my great-grandad Richard Kent wrote on coming home from visiting his brother Eammon Ceannt, executed the following morning. Their brother William was killed near Arras, France, fighting for the British less than a year later. The poem was first performed by Donal O'Kelly, with musicians Dee and Lughaidh Armstrong, at the Sheehy Skeffington Human Rights School 2016.

This lake swallows men, p32
Lough Gara on the Sligo Roscommon border is known for its crannógs and ancient burial sites

Ten so far this morning, p35
A phrase a radio newsreader used brightly, describing that morning's death toll in Gaza.

Hellsteeth, p37
Something my unforgettable friend Bruce Vaughan used to say. The poem is installed in the Hawk's Well Theatre, Sligo. He is also 'The Planter'.

Militant with hope, p37
A line I stole from the poem 'Purse' by Anna Kisby (with her blessing) Her poem is based on the return bus ticket found in the purse of suffragette Emily Davison, who died under the king's horse in 1913.

Early in December, p39
For my grand-aunt Johanna Rose Kent, a.k.a Aunty Tom, Richard's youngest daughter. She lived in their family home in Cabra, the subject of the poem 'In Time'.

ASIMO on prime time TV, p49
Written after an episode of 'QI' which featured the humanoid robot 'Asimo'. The guest was Jo Brand. This was just before the unleashing of military drones on populations around the world.

To the Oxford University Press, p51
A response to the removal of selected words from their Junior Dictionary, to make room for new words. Specifically, the removal of nature to allow for technology.

At the seaside, p55
A pantoum about children being jailed or killed for the crime of throwing stones at armoured tanks in Palestine.

Féis, p58
An Irish-dancing competition.

Great, p61
A response to the centenary celebrations of World War I.

Fusebox, p70
Small disclaimer, I personally never used the broom.

Tourists, p74
The Viking Boat is an amphibious tour bus/boat that rolls around Dublin.

Fracture, p75
Fracking, currently blocked in the south of Ireland.

Dead language, p77
Irish translation by Rossa Ó Snodaigh.

Old woman, p82
My version of the Lazic poem 'I'll be a Wicked Old Woman'.

Acknowledgements

I would like to thank the following:

The editors and staff of the publications where these poems previously appeared: *Abridged, Skylight47, New Irish Writing (The Irish Times* and *The Irish Independent), The Stinging Fly, Shot Glass Journal, Muse-Pie Press, Poetry New Zealand, Ink Sweat & Tears, Ropes, The Stony Thursday Book, Stanzas, Bray Arts Journal, Poetry N.I Poetry Day 2018* chapbook, *Poethead, Bogman's Canon, The Roscommon Herald, Crannóg, Leaf Books, Voices From the Cave, Strokestown Poetry Anthology, Black Light Engine Room Press, North West Words, Agenda, Tridae, Burning Bush 2, The Galway Review, The Cormorant,* and *The Poet's Republic.*

The Francis Ledwidge award, the iYeats poetry competition, and Poetry Ireland Butler's Café competition, who gave first prizes to "Silver Spoon," "Hellsteeth," and "Meet me for coffee." And the Comórtas Filíochta Chultúrlann Ó Fiaich which gave the Irish translation of "Welcome" (translated by Oilí Diarmuid) a first prize.

The Hennessy Literary Award, Galway Hospital Trust's Poems for Patience, Poetry Ireland Love Your Bike competition, Red Line Book Festival poetry competition, Leaf Books, Cúirt New Writing, Bradshaw Books manuscript competition, and Over the Edge New Writer of the Year, which shortlisted poems, including "Hunting in the bathroom," "Tourists," "Welcome," "Backcarrier," "Jamie's red yo-yo," "There was no funeral," "Surprise," "This lake swallows men," "Organic," "Old woman," and "My house."

For reading through this at manuscript stage, my sincere gratitude to Una Mannion, Alice Lyons, Jane Robinson, and specially Neil Young. It's not often you can say your poems made someone's eyes bleed.

For collaborating with me on The Stranger shadow-puppet film-poem, huge thanks and squeals of pride to Carmel Balfe, Helen B. Grehan and Aoife ní Mhurchadha.

Thanks also to Gerry Boland, Melissa Newman, Mary Mullins, Brian McHugh, and the IT Sligo Writing & Literature programme, who all work wonders in the west. And of course Jessie Lendennie and Siobhán Hutson at Salmon Poetry.

Fionnuala O'Connor, for her relentless support.

Too many to mention, sorry. Friends, Hermits, writers, classmates, tutors, family.

And Roj.

This beautiful cover, and all the artwork within the book, are original paintings by Helen Chantrell, a fabulous friend as well as a gifted artist.

Photo: Roisín Loughrey

JESSAMINE O'CONNOR grew up in Dublin and moved to the west of Ireland in 1999 where she now lives in an old train station on the Sligo Roscommon border.

She is recipient of the Francis Ledwidge award, and winner of the iYeats and Poetry Ireland Butler's Café competitions. Her work has been shortlisted at the Doolin Writer's Weekend, Over the Edge New Writer of the Year, Cúirt New Writing, Red Line Book Festival, Dead Good Poetry, Westport Literary Festival and Hennessy Literary Awards.

Her short film, The Stranger, was shortlisted for the 2019 O'Bhéal International Poetry Film Competition. Publications include *The Stinging Fly, Poetry New Zealand, The North, The Ofi Press, One, Shot Glass Journal, Abridged, Fifth Estate, The Poet's Republic, The Cormorant, Ink Sweat & Tears* and *New Irish Writing*; and anthologies such as *Culture Matters, Yeats 150, The Colour of Saying*, and *Strokestown Poetry Festival Anthology*. She has published several chapbooks including one with The Black Light Engine Room press. This is her first collection.

salmonpoetry

Cliffs of Moher, County Clare, Ireland

"Like the sea-run Steelhead salmon that thrashes upstream to its spawning ground, then instead of dying, returns to the sea—Salmon Poetry Press brings precious cargo to both Ireland and America in the poetry it publishes, then carries that select work to its readership against incalculable odds."

TESS GALLAGHER

The Salmon Bookshop
& Literary Centre

Ennistymon, County Clare, Ireland

"Another wonderful Clare outlet."
The Irish Times, 35 Best Independent Bookshops